JESUS at the Temple

Luke 2:22-52

Retold by Pamela Broughton
Illustrated by Joy Friedman

A GOLDEN BOOK® • NEW YORK

Copyright © 1999 Golden Books Publishing Company, Inc. Illustrations © 1986 by Joy Friedman.
All rights reserved. Printed in the U.S.A. No part of this book may be reproduced or copied in any form without
written permission from the publisher. GOLDEN BOOKS®, A GOLDEN BOOK®, and G DESIGN® are
trademarks of Golden Books Publishing Company, Inc., New York, New York, 10106.

After Jesus was born, Mary and Joseph took the baby to Jerusalem, to present him to the Lord at the great Temple there.

There was a man in Jerusalem named Simeon. God had told Simeon that he would see God's special Son before he died.

When Mary and Joseph brought Jesus to the Temple, Simeon was there.

Simeon took Jesus into his arms. He knew that Jesus was God's Son.

He said, "Now, Lord, I will die in peace. You have sent one who will save the lost people of our land."

Then Simeon blessed Mary and Joseph. He gave Jesus back to them.

An old widow named Anna was also in the Temple.
Anna came up to Mary and Joseph, and thanked God.

She told everyone that God's Son had come.

When they had done everything according to the
law of God, Mary and Joseph took Jesus and returned
to Nazareth, their home in Galilee.

The child grew and became strong. And his wisdom and understanding grew, too.

When Jesus was twelve years old, his parents again
took him to Jerusalem. This time they went to
celebrate the Feast of Passover at the Temple.

After celebrating for seven days, Mary and Joseph set out for home. But Jesus stayed behind.

Jesus's parents did not know this. They thought he was traveling home with some others who were also returning to Nazareth.

But after they had gone a day's journey, they began to look for him.

They could not find him there. So they went all the way back to Jerusalem to look for him.

After three days of searching, they finally found
him in the Temple. Jesus was sitting with the teachers,
listening to them and asking them questions.

All who heard him were amazed at his understanding and wisdom.

When his parents found him, Mary said, "Son, why have you treated us so? We have been trying to find you, and we've been terribly worried."

"Why were you looking for me?" Jesus asked. "Did you not know I would stay here at the Temple, doing my Father's business?"

His parents did not understand his words.

But Jesus returned to Nazareth with them, and was an obedient son.

Mary lovingly kept all these things in her heart.

Jesus grew tall and wise, and was loved by God and man.